MELBOURNE AUSTRALIA TRAVEL GUIDE 2025

A Dynamic Blend of Art, Nature, and Urban Adventure

SHARRON CARTER

Copyright

© **2024 Sharron Carter**

All rights reserved.

This document may not be replicated or reproduced in any form without permission from the publisher.

As a result, the information inside cannot be transferred, stored electronically, or maintained in a database.

The publisher or creator must give their consent before any part of the document may be copied, scanned, faxed, or kept.

TABLE OF CONTENTS

TABLE OF CONTENTS
1.0 Introduction to Melbourne
　　Overview of Melbourne: History, Culture, and Identity
　　Why Visit Melbourne in 2025: What's New and What's Timeless
　　The City's Art, Music, and Culinary Scene
　　Essential Travel Information: Best Time to Visit, Weather, and Festivals
　　Key Facts: Transportation, Currency, and Local Etiquette
2.0 Getting to and Around Melbourne
　　Arriving in Melbourne: Airports, Flights, and Transportation Options
　　Getting Around the City: Trains, Trams, Buses, and Ride-Sharing
　　Cycling Around Melbourne: Bike-Friendly Streets and Rental Services
　　Car Rental and Driving Tips: Navigating Melbourne and Beyond
　　Day Trips and Excursions from Melbourne: How to Explore the Surrounding Areas
3.0 Iconic Landmarks and Attractions
　　Federation Square: Melbourne's Cultural Heart
　　Royal Botanic Gardens: Nature and Relaxation in the City
　　Eureka Skydeck: Stunning Views of Melbourne's Skyline
　　Melbourne Zoo: Wildlife Experiences and

Conservation Efforts

Queen Victoria Market: Melbourne's Largest Outdoor Market

Melbourne Museum and IMAX: Exploring Art, Science, and History

4.0 Arts, Culture, and Entertainment

Melbourne's Laneways and Street Art: Hidden Gems of Creativity

National Gallery of Victoria (NGV): Art Collections and Exhibitions

Melbourne's Theatre Scene: Theatres, Shows, and Festivals

Live Music Venues: Exploring Melbourne's Vibrant Music Culture

Cultural Festivals: Melbourne International Comedy Festival, Melbourne International Film Festival, and More

Art Galleries and Independent Studios: Discovering Local Talent

5.0 Dining and Nightlife in Melbourne

Best Restaurants in Melbourne: Fine Dining, Local Favorites, and Hidden Gems

Melbourne's Café Culture: Best Spots for Coffee and Brunch

Street Food and Food Trucks: Where to Find Authentic Melbourne Eats

Wine, Cocktails, and Breweries: Melbourne's Bar and Nightlife Scene

Vegetarian, Vegan, and Gluten-Free Dining: Best Places for Plant-Based Cuisine

Late-Night Dining: Where to Eat After Hours in

Melbourne

6.0 Shopping in Melbourne

    Melbourne's Shopping Districts: Bourke Street Mall, Chapel Street, and Fitzroy

    High-End Shopping: Designer Boutiques and Flagship Stores

    Vintage and Second-Hand Stores: Unique Finds and Sustainable Shopping

    Melbourne's Best Markets: Queen Victoria Market, South Melbourne Market, and Prahran Market

    Australian Souvenirs: What to Buy and Where to Find It

    Fashion and Design: Melbourne as a Hub for Australian Fashion

7.0 Melbourne's Neighborhoods and Hidden Gems

    Exploring Melbourne's Inner Suburbs: Fitzroy, Collingwood, and Carlton

    St Kilda: The Beachside Village with a Bohemian Vibe

    Southbank and South Melbourne: The Cultural and Dining Heart of the City

    Docklands: Modern Shopping, Dining, and Entertainment

    North Melbourne and Kensington: Off-the-Beaten-Path Neighborhoods

8.0 Day Trips and Excursions from Melbourne

    Great Ocean Road: Scenic Drives, Beaches, and the Twelve Apostles

    Phillip Island: Penguins, Wildlife, and Family-Friendly Fun

    Yarra Valley: Wine Tours, Vineyards, and Scenic

    Views

    Mornington Peninsula: Beaches, Hot Springs, and Hiking Trails

    Grampians National Park: Hiking, Wildlife, and Nature Escapes

    Wilson's Promontory: Pristine Beaches, Wildlife, and Hiking Trails

    Conclusion

9.0 Family-Friendly Activities in Melbourne

    Melbourne Zoo and Healesville Sanctuary: Wildlife Encounters for All Ages

    Scienceworks: Interactive Exhibits for Kids and Families

    Melbourne Star Observation Wheel: A Fun Family Experience

    Family-Friendly Parks: Royal Park, Fitzroy Gardens, and the Melbourne Botanic Gardens

    Indoor Activities for Families: Trampolining, Bowling, and Ice Skating

    Kid-Friendly Cafés and Restaurants: Dining Spots for Young Families

    Conclusion

10.0 Practical Information and Travel Tips

    Currency, ATMs, and Payment Methods:

    Health and Safety:

    Language and Communication:

    Using Public Transport:

    Internet Access and SIM Cards:

    Sustainability and Responsible Travel:

1.0 Introduction to Melbourne

Overview of Melbourne: History, Culture, and Identity

Melbourne, often regarded as Australia's cultural capital, is a vibrant, multicultural city that has evolved into one of the world's most dynamic urban centers. Located in the southeastern corner of the Australian continent, Melbourne is the capital of the state of Victoria. Established in 1835, the city's history is rooted in its early days as a British settlement, growing rapidly during the Victorian gold rush of the 1850s. This wealth transformed Melbourne into a cosmopolitan hub, with grand Victorian architecture and cultural institutions that still define the city today.

Over the years, Melbourne has built its identity as a cultural and artistic mecca, known for its eclectic mix of modern urbanism and historical charm. The city's love for arts, fashion, food, and music is reflected in every corner, from its laneways adorned with street art to its renowned galleries and theaters. It is a city that celebrates diversity, with a rich blend of cultures contributing to its dynamic atmosphere.

Why Visit Melbourne in 2025: What's New and What's Timeless

In 2025, Melbourne continues to be a must-visit destination for travelers seeking a blend of the new and timeless. The city remains a global hotspot for art lovers, foodies, and urban explorers, offering something for everyone. The Melbourne International Comedy Festival, Melbourne International Film Festival, and Melbourne Fashion

Week continue to be major attractions, showcasing the city's thriving creative scene.

New developments in 2025 further enhance Melbourne's appeal. The city's ever-evolving waterfront, including the Southbank precinct, has seen the opening of cutting-edge restaurants, luxury accommodations, and art installations. Additionally, Melbourne's investment in sustainability is visible through initiatives such as green spaces, bike-friendly lanes, and environmentally conscious architecture.

Timeless attractions, such as the iconic Royal Botanic Gardens, the National Gallery of Victoria, and the historic Queen Victoria Market, continue to attract visitors from around the world. The city's famous laneways, like Hosier Lane, still offer a taste of its artistic soul, while Federation Square remains a central gathering place for locals and tourists alike.

The City's Art, Music, and Culinary Scene

Melbourne's cultural scene is its beating heart. It is home to world-class museums and galleries, including the NGV (National Gallery of Victoria), which houses a rich collection of international and Australian art. Melbourne is also known for its vibrant street art culture, with laneways like ACDC Lane and Hosier Lane showcasing ever-changing murals and graffiti art.

The city's music scene is equally eclectic, offering everything from classical performances at the Melbourne Symphony Orchestra to indie gigs at The Espy or The Corner Hotel. Melbourne's reputation as a live music hub is cemented by its range of music festivals, including Moomba and Live at the Bowl, which feature local and international talent.

When it comes to food, Melbourne is a paradise for culinary enthusiasts. The city's multicultural heritage shines through in its diverse dining options, from Asian street food in Chinatown to Italian eateries in Lygon Street. Melbourne is also famous for its coffee culture, with cafes dotted throughout the city offering artisanal brews that rival the best in the world. For fine dining, Melbourne boasts several Michelin-starred restaurants and critically acclaimed chefs, making it a destination for gastronomic adventures.

Essential Travel Information: Best Time to Visit, Weather, and Festivals

The best time to visit Melbourne is during the spring (September to November) or autumn (March to May) months. These seasons offer mild temperatures, making it perfect for exploring the city's outdoor attractions. Summer (December to

February) is warm and lively, with outdoor festivals and events, but can also get quite hot, with temperatures occasionally exceeding 35°C (95°F). Winter (June to August) can be cold and unpredictable, with temperatures often hovering around 10°C (50°F), but this is the best time for indoor cultural experiences like visiting museums and enjoying Melbourne's famous coffee.

Melbourne is also known for its festivals throughout the year, including the Melbourne International Arts Festival, Melbourne Food and Wine Festival, and White Night Melbourne, a citywide event where art and culture fill the streets with light, music, and performance.

Key Facts: Transportation, Currency, and Local Etiquette

Melbourne is well-served by public transportation, with an extensive network of trams, buses, and trains making it easy to get around. The city's iconic tram system is free within the Central Business District (CBD), and the myki card is used for travel on all public transport outside the free zone. For those looking to explore the surroundings, Melbourne Airport connects to international and domestic flights, and V/Line trains offer access to regional areas.

Melbourne's currency is the Australian Dollar (AUD), and while credit and debit cards are widely accepted, it's a good idea to have some cash on hand for small purchases or local markets. Tipping is not compulsory in Australia, but it is appreciated for excellent service in restaurants and cafes.

In terms of local etiquette, Australians are known for their casual and friendly demeanor. It's common to address people by their first names, and tipping is generally not expected, although leaving a small tip for good service is a nice gesture. When visiting public spaces, be mindful of local norms regarding quietness in libraries, respectful behavior in galleries, and patience in queues—all of which contribute to Melbourne's laid-back yet courteous atmosphere.

In conclusion, Melbourne is a city that offers an endless array of cultural, culinary, and artistic experiences. Whether you're drawn to the timeless charm of its historic streets or the cutting-edge innovations of its urban scene, Melbourne in 2025 promises an unforgettable experience for any traveler.

2.0 Getting to and Around Melbourne

Arriving in Melbourne: Airports, Flights, and Transportation Options

Melbourne is a major international gateway, with several convenient options for travelers flying in. The city's main international and domestic hub is Melbourne Airport (Tullamarine), located 23 kilometers (14 miles) north of the city center. This airport offers direct flights from major cities worldwide, including routes from Asia, Europe, the Americas, and New Zealand. Melbourne Airport is well-equipped with all the modern amenities, including duty-free shopping, cafes, and lounges. Upon arrival, travelers can easily access the city center by taxi, private car, or public transport.

The SkyBus offers a convenient and affordable shuttle service from the airport to Southern Cross Station in Melbourne's central business district (CBD). The trip takes around 20-30 minutes, depending on traffic. Alternatively, visitors can take a taxi or use ride-sharing apps like Uber or Ola to reach the city. For those arriving on domestic flights, Avalon Airport is another option, though it is located further out from the city (50 kilometers or 31 miles south) and primarily serves low-cost carriers.

Getting Around the City: Trains, Trams, Buses, and Ride-Sharing

Melbourne has an extensive and efficient public transportation network, making it easy to explore the city and its surrounding areas. The train system connects the city to suburban areas and regional destinations, with trains running frequently from major stations like Southern Cross Station and

Flinders Street Station. Trains are a great option for exploring Melbourne's suburbs or taking day trips to nearby destinations like the Yarra Valley or Geelong.

The iconic tram network is another key feature of Melbourne's public transport. Trams are an integral part of the city's charm, with over 250 routes crisscrossing Melbourne. Within the city center, trams are free to ride in the Free Tram Zone, which covers the main shopping, dining, and tourist areas. For travel beyond this zone, visitors can use a myki card, a smartcard that works on trains, trams, and buses throughout Melbourne.

Melbourne's bus system complements the train and tram network, connecting areas that may not be served by other forms of transport. Buses are especially useful for reaching more remote suburbs or parks. As with trams and trains, the myki card is required to travel on buses.

For those preferring private transportation, ride-sharing services like Uber, Ola, and Didi are widely available across the city. These services offer a convenient and cashless way to get around Melbourne, with apps providing real-time tracking and price estimates.

Cycling Around Melbourne: Bike-Friendly Streets and Rental Services

Melbourne is one of the most bike-friendly cities in Australia, with an increasing number of dedicated bike lanes and cycling paths. Whether you want to explore the city's neighborhoods or venture into its many parks, cycling is a great option for getting around. Melbourne's bike lanes connect many of the city's top destinations, and several inner-city streets, such as Carlton, Fitzroy, and St Kilda, are particularly popular with cyclists.

For those who don't have their own bike, there are several bike rental services available. Melbourne Bike Share offers a fleet of bikes for short-term rentals, and there are also independent bike rental shops where you can rent bikes for longer periods. You can use these bikes to explore the Yarra River Trail, Albert Park, or the Royal Botanic Gardens—all of which offer beautiful cycling routes.

Car Rental and Driving Tips: Navigating Melbourne and Beyond

Although Melbourne has excellent public transport, some visitors may prefer to rent a car to explore the city or venture further into regional Victoria. Car rental is available at Melbourne Airport as well as in the city center. Renting a car gives you the flexibility to explore nearby attractions such as the Great

Ocean Road, Phillip Island, or the Dandenong Ranges.

When driving in Melbourne, it's important to keep in mind that Australia uses left-hand side driving. Major roads are well-maintained, and Melbourne's road network is easy to navigate, with clear signs and well-marked intersections. Parking can be challenging in the city center, and street parking may require paying through parking meters or parking apps. There are also plenty of secure car parks throughout the CBD and at popular tourist destinations.

Day Trips and Excursions from Melbourne: How to Explore the Surrounding Areas

Melbourne is perfectly situated for day trips and excursions to a variety of scenic and historic locations. One of the most popular destinations is the Great Ocean Road, which takes you along the stunning southern coastline, offering views of the Twelve Apostles and charming seaside towns like Lorne and Apollo Bay. This route is easily accessible by car, and there are also guided bus tours available.

For wine lovers, the Yarra Valley is a short drive from Melbourne and offers an array of vineyards and wineries. You can enjoy wine tastings and gourmet food in this lush region, which is also home to charming villages like Healesville and Warburton.

Another excellent day trip option is Phillip Island, known for its Penguin Parade and pristine beaches. The island is accessible by car or bus from Melbourne, and it's a great spot for wildlife watching, as well as enjoying the coastal scenery.

Lastly, nature lovers can head to the Dandenong Ranges, which is only about an hour from the city. Here, you can enjoy walking trails, visit quaint towns like Olinda and Mount Dandenong, and take a scenic ride on the Puffing Billy Railway, a historic steam train.

Overall, Melbourne offers a variety of ways to get around the city and explore the surrounding regions, whether by public transport, bike, car, or organized tours. Each option provides flexibility and convenience, making it easy to discover everything this exciting city and its beautiful surroundings have to offer.

3.0 Iconic Landmarks and Attractions

Federation Square: Melbourne's Cultural Heart

Federation Square is one of Melbourne's most iconic and vibrant spaces, acting as the cultural heart of the city. Located in the CBD, this urban precinct is a hub for art, architecture, and public events. The square itself is home to a mix of modern and historical architecture, with the contemporary design of the Ian Potter Centre and ACMI (Australian Centre for the Moving Image) standing alongside more traditional landmarks. Federation Square is a popular gathering spot for locals and tourists alike, offering a wealth of cultural experiences, from exhibitions to live performances and festivals. Visitors can explore the galleries, dine in the many cafes and restaurants, or enjoy outdoor events in the plaza. With its proximity to the Flinders Street Station and other central attractions, Federation Square is an essential stop for anyone visiting Melbourne.

Royal Botanic Gardens: Nature and Relaxation in the City

The Royal Botanic Gardens, located in the heart of Melbourne, offer a peaceful escape from the hustle and bustle of city life. This expansive garden is one of the most beautiful green spaces in the city, spanning 38 hectares along the Yarra River. With its lush lawns, tranquil lakes, and diverse plant species, it's a haven for nature lovers and those looking to relax. The gardens are home to over 8,500 plant species from around the world, making it a botanical paradise. Visitors can enjoy leisurely walks through themed areas such as the Herb Garden and Fern Gully, take a boat ride on the

Lake, or simply relax under the trees. The Gardens' Visitor Centre offers guided tours and educational programs for those interested in learning more about the flora. The Royal Botanic Gardens also hosts various events throughout the year, including outdoor cinema screenings, music performances, and yoga sessions.

Eureka Skydeck: Stunning Views of Melbourne's Skyline

For breathtaking panoramic views of Melbourne, a visit to the Eureka Skydeck is a must. Located on the 88th floor of the Eureka Tower in Southbank, the Skydeck offers sweeping views of the city, Port Phillip Bay, and beyond. The 360-degree observation deck is one of the highest public viewing points in the Southern Hemisphere. Visitors can take in the impressive skyline, spot landmarks such as the Melbourne Cricket Ground and

Federation Square, and marvel at the expansive landscape stretching towards the bay. For an even more thrilling experience, the Edge Experience allows visitors to step into a glass cube that projects out from the building, offering an exhilarating view of the city below. The Eureka Skydeck is particularly stunning at sunset or during the night when Melbourne's lights come alive.

Melbourne Zoo: Wildlife Experiences and Conservation Efforts

The Melbourne Zoo is one of Australia's oldest and most renowned zoological parks, offering visitors the chance to experience wildlife from around the globe. Located just 4 km from the city center, the zoo spans 55 acres and is home to over 300 species of animals. The zoo is divided into themed areas, including Gorilla Rainforest, Wild Sea, and The Outback, where visitors can see iconic

Australian animals like kangaroos and koalas alongside international species such as tigers, elephants, and giraffes. The zoo is dedicated to conservation, participating in breeding programs and wildlife protection efforts. One of its most popular features is the Animal Encounters Program, where guests can get up close to certain animals and learn about their behaviors and habitats. Whether you're a wildlife enthusiast or a family with children, Melbourne Zoo offers an engaging and educational experience.

Queen Victoria Market: Melbourne's Largest Outdoor Market

Queen Victoria Market is a Melbourne institution and the city's largest outdoor market. Situated just north of the CBD, this bustling market is an essential stop for anyone looking to experience local food, shopping, and culture. The market has a history dating back to the 19th century and is renowned for its vibrant atmosphere and diverse range of stalls. Visitors can find everything from fresh produce, gourmet food, and artisanal products to clothing, homewares, and souvenirs. The Deli Hall is famous for its variety of cheeses, meats, and baked goods, while the fruit and vegetable stalls offer the best of Melbourne's seasonal produce. The market is also home to various food trucks, eateries, and cafes, making it a great spot for enjoying a bite to eat. The Queen Victoria Market also hosts night markets and seasonal events, providing a lively cultural experience for both locals and tourists.

Melbourne Museum and IMAX: Exploring Art, Science, and History

The Melbourne Museum is one of the largest and most engaging museums in Australia, offering exhibits that span art, science, history, and culture. Located in Carlton Gardens, the museum features a wide range of permanent collections and temporary exhibitions, making it a must-visit for anyone interested in learning more about Melbourne and the world beyond. Highlights include the Bunjilaka Aboriginal Cultural Centre, which showcases indigenous culture, and the Megalodon Exhibit, which houses an impressive display of prehistoric creatures. The museum is also home to the IMAX Theatre, one of the largest screens in the Southern Hemisphere, offering a state-of-the-art cinema experience. With its interactive displays, rich collections, and educational programs, the Melbourne Museum provides a fascinating look into the natural world, human history, and cultural heritage.

Melbourne's iconic landmarks and attractions showcase the city's diverse character and rich history. From the cultural richness of Federation Square to the tranquil beauty of the Royal Botanic Gardens and the thrilling heights of the Eureka Skydeck, there is something for every type of traveler in this vibrant city.

4.0 Arts, Culture, and Entertainment

Melbourne's Laneways and Street Art: Hidden Gems of Creativity

Melbourne is renowned for its vibrant street art culture, and the city's laneways provide an open-air canvas for artists from around the world. Wander through iconic laneways like Hosier Lane, AC/DC Lane, and Duckboard Place, where walls are adorned with colorful murals, graffiti, and stencil art. These hidden pockets of creativity are constantly evolving, with new artworks frequently replacing old ones, making each visit a unique experience. The laneways not only showcase Melbourne's creative spirit but also reflect the city's urban transformation, where street art is celebrated as legitimate artistic expression. Walking tours are available for those who want a deeper understanding of the artists and the stories behind the works. The laneways are also home to quirky cafes, boutiques, and galleries, making them a perfect fusion of art, culture, and city life.

National Gallery of Victoria (NGV): Art Collections and Exhibitions

The National Gallery of Victoria (NGV) is Australia's oldest and most visited public art museum, housing a world-class collection of over 70,000 works of art. Located on St. Kilda Road, the NGV is divided into two major spaces: the NGV International, which showcases European, Asian, and international art, and the Ian Potter Centre, which focuses on Australian art. The NGV offers a rich variety of permanent and temporary exhibitions, from classical masterpieces to contemporary works. It is known for hosting high-profile exhibitions, including retrospectives of global artists and exhibitions of cutting-edge contemporary art. The gallery's architecture is equally impressive, with the NGV International featuring an iconic glass atrium and the serene Waterwall that serves as a striking entryway. With free entry to its permanent collections and discounted or free access to temporary exhibits, the NGV is a cultural treasure trove that should not be missed.

Melbourne's Theatre Scene: Theatres, Shows, and Festivals

Melbourne boasts a thriving theatre scene, offering a range of performances from world-class productions to experimental and independent theatre. The Arts Precinct, located near Southbank, is home to many of the city's major theatres, including the Melbourne Theatre Company (MTC), the State Theatre, and Her Majesty's Theatre.

These venues host everything from classic Shakespearean plays to contemporary dramas, musicals, and Australian works. In addition to the major theatres, Melbourne is home to a thriving independent theatre scene, with smaller venues like The Malthouse Theatre and The Forum Theatre showcasing experimental and avant-garde performances. The city's commitment to theatre is further highlighted during annual festivals like Midsumma Festival and Melbourne International Comedy Festival, which celebrate a range of theatrical genres. Whether you're a fan of large-scale productions or intimate performances, Melbourne's theatre scene offers something for everyone.

Live Music Venues: Exploring Melbourne's Vibrant Music Culture

Melbourne's live music scene is legendary, and the city is known for its diverse range of music venues, from intimate pubs to grand concert halls. Iconic venues like The Corner Hotel in Richmond, The Tote in Collingwood, and Cherry Bar in AC/DC Lane offer a platform for local and international acts to perform across a variety of genres, including rock, jazz, indie, and electronic. For a larger-than-life experience, head to the Forum Theatre or Rod Laver Arena for big-name concerts and events. The city's music culture is deeply rooted in its alternative scene, and Melbourne regularly hosts music festivals such as Moomba Festival, Melbourne International Jazz Festival, and The St Kilda Festival, which celebrate both local talent and international acts. Whether you're after a relaxed acoustic performance or a high-energy concert,

Melbourne's live music venues are the heartbeat of the city's nightlife.

Cultural Festivals: Melbourne International Comedy Festival, Melbourne International Film Festival, and More

Melbourne is home to a vibrant cultural calendar, with numerous festivals taking place throughout the year. The Melbourne International Comedy Festival is one of the largest and most well-known comedy festivals in the world, attracting comedians from all over the globe for a month-long celebration of laughter. Held annually in March and April, the festival features stand-up performances, improv shows, and theatre productions at venues across the city. For film enthusiasts, the Melbourne International Film Festival (MIFF), held in August, showcases the best of international cinema, including both well-established filmmakers and emerging talent. In addition to these, Melbourne hosts a variety of cultural events such as White Night, Melbourne Fringe Festival, and Melbourne Food and Wine Festival, all of which highlight the city's creative spirit. These festivals not only bring together artists and performers but also offer unique experiences for visitors to enjoy the city's dynamic cultural scene.

Art Galleries and Independent Studios: Discovering Local Talent

While Melbourne is home to world-class institutions like the NGV, the city is also a hub for independent art galleries and studios that showcase the work of local and emerging artists. The Australian Centre for Contemporary Art (ACCA) in South Melbourne is a leading contemporary art space, presenting cutting-edge exhibitions that challenge conventional artistic boundaries. The Blender Gallery and Streeton Gallery focus on Australian contemporary and modern art, while smaller spaces like Gertrude Contemporary and Tin Sheds provide a platform for experimental and multidisciplinary works. Melbourne is also home to a thriving independent studio scene, where artists work in converted warehouses and studios. Many of these artists open their doors to the public during events like Open House Melbourne and Art Melbourne, allowing visitors to get an exclusive glimpse into the creative process. These independent galleries and studios reflect the city's passion for innovation, and they offer a great opportunity to explore Melbourne's local talent and artistic diversity.

Melbourne's arts, culture, and entertainment scene is an eclectic blend of world-class institutions and local creativity. From the vibrant street art in laneways to iconic museums, live music venues, and a wealth of cultural festivals, the city offers endless opportunities to experience the best of

Australian and international culture. Whether you're attending a theatre performance, exploring an art gallery, or enjoying a music festival, Melbourne is a cultural capital that celebrates creativity in all its forms.

5.0 Dining and Nightlife in Melbourne

Best Restaurants in Melbourne: Fine Dining, Local Favorites, and Hidden Gems

Melbourne is a food lover's paradise, offering a diverse range of dining experiences, from sophisticated fine dining to hidden local gems. The city's top fine dining venues, such as Attica in Ripponlea, renowned for its modern Australian cuisine and creative dishes, and Cutler & Co. in Fitzroy, offer world-class service and exceptional culinary experiences. For those seeking local favorites, Chin Chin in the CBD is a popular spot for contemporary Thai dishes, while Flower Drum offers Cantonese delicacies. Melbourne also has its fair share of hidden gems, such as Ishizuka, an intimate Japanese restaurant in Collins Street serving kaiseki, or Supernormal, where you can enjoy a unique fusion of Asian flavors. Whether you're craving refined elegance or a laid-back neighborhood vibe, Melbourne's dining scene offers something for everyone.

Melbourne's Café Culture: Best Spots for Coffee and Brunch

Melbourne's café culture is an integral part of the city's identity, and it's no surprise that locals take their coffee seriously. From trendy spots to cozy neighborhood cafes, the city has some of the best coffee in the world. St. Ali in South Melbourne is a pioneering café in the third-wave coffee movement, known for its expert brewing and innovative menu. Proud Mary in Collingwood is another must-visit, offering high-quality coffee and delicious brunch options. Melbourne's brunch scene is also exceptional, with cafes like Higher Ground serving inventive dishes in a stylish setting, and Hardware Société in the CBD offering a French-inspired brunch menu. Whether you're in the mood for a simple flat white or an elaborate avocado toast, Melbourne's cafés provide a delightful experience for coffee lovers and brunch enthusiasts alike.

Street Food and Food Trucks: Where to Find Authentic Melbourne Eats

For those who prefer casual dining, Melbourne's vibrant street food scene offers an exciting way to explore local flavors. Queen Victoria Market is a hub for food trucks and street food vendors, offering everything from Asian dumplings to gourmet burgers and Mexican tacos. The Night Noodle Markets in the summer bring together a dazzling array of food trucks serving up Asian street food staples like bao, satay, and ramen. South

Melbourne Market is another great spot for street food lovers, offering delicious treats like freshly made dim sum, hot chips, and Greek souvlaki. Melbourne's street food scene is a reflection of the city's multicultural vibe, and it's the perfect way to sample a variety of flavors on the go.

Wine, Cocktails, and Breweries: Melbourne's Bar and Nightlife Scene

Melbourne's nightlife is just as diverse as its dining scene, with an array of bars, pubs, and nightclubs catering to all tastes. For wine lovers, Fitzroy's Bar Clara offers an intimate atmosphere with an extensive wine list, while City Wine Shop is a great place for a glass of wine and a bite to eat in the heart of the city. Cocktail enthusiasts will enjoy The Everleigh, an iconic Melbourne bar that serves expertly crafted cocktails in a vintage setting, or Black Pearl in Fitzroy, known for its innovative drinks and laid-back ambiance. Melbourne's craft beer scene has also been booming, with breweries like Stomping Ground Brewery in Collingwood and BrewDog in the CBD offering unique brews and a fun atmosphere for beer lovers. The city's nightlife is as vibrant as its food scene, with plenty of spots to unwind after dark.

Vegetarian, Vegan, and Gluten-Free Dining: Best Places for Plant-Based Cuisine

Melbourne is a fantastic city for plant-based eaters, with an abundance of vegetarian, vegan, and gluten-free options. Transformer Fitzroy offers an inventive vegan menu with dishes like smoked carrot with hummus and grains, while Smith & Daughters in Fitzroy serves plant-based dishes inspired by global flavors. For those with dietary restrictions, Shakahari in Carlton has been serving up vegetarian and vegan Indian dishes for decades. Gluten-free diners can enjoy delicious offerings at Fitzrovia or Café Who in the CBD, both of which specialize in gluten-free menus. Melbourne's commitment to inclusive dining means that whether you follow a plant-based, gluten-free, or dairy-free diet, there are plenty of tasty and creative options to explore.

Late-Night Dining: Where to Eat After Hours in Melbourne

For those who find themselves hungry after hours, Melbourne offers a range of late-night dining options. Chin Chin in the CBD is known for its late-night menu, serving Thai-inspired dishes until the early hours of the morning. Rasa Rasa in Fitzroy is another popular late-night eatery, offering Malaysian street food at all hours. For something more casual, Shujinko in the CBD serves up ramen until 4 a.m., making it a favorite for night owls. Melbourne's late-night dining scene is not only about convenience but also about providing quality food to keep the city's lively crowd fueled long into the night.

Melbourne's dining and nightlife scene is a celebration of the city's rich cultural diversity and commitment to innovation. From top-tier restaurants and vibrant street food stalls to thriving café culture and exciting nightlife, Melbourne offers a culinary experience that caters to all tastes and preferences. Whether you're indulging in a fine dining experience, sipping on craft cocktails, or enjoying a late-night ramen, the city's food and drink offerings are an essential part of its dynamic and ever-evolving identity.

6.0 Shopping in Melbourne

Melbourne is a shopper's paradise, offering a wide variety of shopping experiences from high-end designer boutiques to quirky vintage stores and bustling local markets. Whether you're hunting for the latest fashion trends, unique souvenirs, or sustainable shopping options, Melbourne has something to offer every kind of shopper.

Melbourne's Shopping Districts: Bourke Street Mall, Chapel Street, and Fitzroy

Melbourne's shopping districts cater to all tastes and budgets. Bourke Street Mall, located in the heart of the city, is the epicenter of retail, featuring both local and international department stores like Myer and David Jones, as well as popular brands such as H&M and Zara. For those seeking something a little more eclectic, Chapel Street in South Yarra offers a mix of high-end boutiques, vintage stores, and independent fashion retailers, making it one of Melbourne's most fashionable shopping streets. Further out, the Fitzroy area is a hub for Melbourne's hip and alternative fashion scene, with trendy stores showcasing up-and-coming designers, second-hand shops, and streetwear brands. These neighborhoods are perfect for those looking to shop in vibrant, dynamic settings with a local touch.

High-End Shopping: Designer Boutiques and Flagship Stores

For luxury shopping, Melbourne is home to a number of high-end shopping precincts, where you can find designer boutiques and flagship stores. The Collins Street shopping strip is known for its luxury offerings, with high-end brands like Louis Vuitton, Gucci, and Prada occupying elegant, historic buildings. Emporium Melbourne, a sleek and modern shopping center located near the city center, hosts both international designer labels and Australian luxury brands, with boutiques like Chanel and Burberry alongside local luxury labels. Melbourne's Chadstone Shopping Centre, one of the largest shopping centers in the Southern Hemisphere, boasts an impressive collection of luxury brands, making it a must-visit destination for those seeking top-tier fashion and accessories.

Vintage and Second-Hand Stores: Unique Finds and Sustainable Shopping

Melbourne is also a hotspot for vintage shopping and sustainable fashion. Fitzroy is home to some of the city's best vintage and second-hand stores, including RetroStar and Vintage Garage, where you can find pre-loved clothing, accessories, and unique pieces that reflect Melbourne's rich fashion history. Hunter Gatherer in the city offers a curated collection of both vintage and contemporary fashion, while Shag in St. Kilda is another popular destination for retro clothing and accessories. For sustainable shopping, Melbourne has a growing number of eco-conscious boutiques such as The Social Outfit and Slow Fashion Melbourne, where you can purchase high-quality, ethically made clothing that has a minimal impact on the environment.

Melbourne's Best Markets: Queen Victoria Market, South Melbourne Market, and Prahran Market

If you want to explore Melbourne's local culture through its markets, there's no better place to start than Queen Victoria Market. As one of the largest and oldest open-air markets in the Southern Hemisphere, it offers a wide variety of fresh produce, gourmet foods, and local artisan products. The market is also home to a range of fashion and craft stalls, selling everything from handmade jewelry to vintage clothing. For a more laid-back atmosphere, South Melbourne Market is a great destination, known for its food stalls and local artisan goods. Prahran Market, located in the trendy suburb of Prahran, is Melbourne's oldest market, offering a mix of fresh food, local produce, and unique fashion items, perfect for those looking to experience the city's local flavor and style.

Australian Souvenirs: What to Buy and Where to Find It

When it comes to souvenirs, Melbourne offers a wide range of Australian-made goods. Aboriginal art and crafts, such as painted boomerangs, woven baskets, and traditional didgeridoos, are popular items to bring home, with many galleries in the city offering authentic pieces. Australian-made fashion, including woolen scarves, leather goods, and accessories, can be found at local shops like The Koorie Heritage Trust or Country Road. For something more uniquely Melbourne, you might want to visit Federation Square's Australian Design Store, where you can find contemporary Australian designs and products ranging from homewares to jewelry.

Fashion and Design: Melbourne as a Hub for Australian Fashion

Melbourne has long been recognized as a fashion capital, with its vibrant and diverse fashion scene making it a hub for Australian designers. The city hosts major fashion events like Melbourne Fashion Week, where designers showcase the latest trends, and the Australian Fashion Chamber celebrates the work of local talents. Melbourne is home to iconic Australian brands such as Gorman, known for its bold prints and eclectic designs, and Aje, which offers contemporary, art-inspired fashion. Melbourne Central and DFO South Wharf are also great spots to find Australian designer pieces at discounted prices. Melbourne's fashion landscape is diverse, ranging from high-end designers to streetwear, reflecting the city's ever-evolving cultural identity.

Melbourne offers a unique shopping experience that caters to every taste, whether you're seeking luxury items, vintage treasures, sustainable fashion, or local Australian goods. With its eclectic mix of shopping districts, thriving markets, and cutting-edge design scene, the city provides an exceptional blend of style, culture, and creativity, making it a must-visit destination for any fashion lover.

7.0 Melbourne's Neighborhoods and Hidden Gems

Melbourne is a city of distinct neighborhoods, each offering its own unique character, charm, and atmosphere. From the bohemian vibes of Fitzroy to the modernity of Docklands, the city's diverse areas have much to offer for every kind of traveler. Whether you're looking for vibrant street art, a quiet park to unwind, or the perfect café to sip a coffee, Melbourne's neighborhoods and hidden gems are waiting to be explored.

Exploring Melbourne's Inner Suburbs: Fitzroy, Collingwood, and Carlton

Melbourne's inner suburbs, such as Fitzroy, Collingwood, and Carlton, are at the heart of the city's creative and cultural scene. Fitzroy is known for its edgy, alternative vibe with its eclectic mix of independent boutiques, vintage stores, and street art. The Rose Street Artists' Market is a great place to find locally-made art and crafts, while Brunswick Street is lined with hip bars, cafés, and eateries. Just a short walk away, Collingwood has seen a revival in recent years, now home to creative hubs and innovative cafés, as well as an increasing number of designer shops and galleries. Carlton, known as Melbourne's "Little Italy," offers a wonderful blend of Italian heritage, from its fantastic Italian restaurants and cafés to its charming Victorian architecture. The Carlton Gardens, home to the Royal Exhibition Building and the Melbourne Museum, is a peaceful spot to enjoy a picnic.

St Kilda: The Beachside Village with a Bohemian Vibe

Located just a short tram ride from the city center, St Kilda is Melbourne's iconic beachside neighborhood, known for its bohemian atmosphere, lively atmosphere, and laid-back vibe. The St Kilda Pier offers stunning views of the city skyline and the bay, and the area is popular for walking, cycling, and kite surfing. Acland Street, lined with cafés, restaurants, and vintage shops, is the perfect spot for a leisurely stroll. Don't forget to visit Luna Park, an historic amusement park with a giant mouth entrance that has been an integral part of Melbourne's cultural history. St Kilda also boasts a vibrant nightlife scene, with a range of pubs, clubs, and beach bars that stay open into the late hours. The St Kilda Foreshore is perfect for a relaxing afternoon, with plenty of picnic areas, walking tracks, and stunning sunset views.

Southbank and South Melbourne: The Cultural and Dining Heart of the City

The Southbank area is Melbourne's cultural and dining hub, home to the National Gallery of Victoria (NGV), Arts Centre Melbourne, and Melbourne Recital Centre. This area is known for its impressive architecture and vibrant cultural offerings, making it a must-visit for art lovers. Southbank Promenade is lined with cafés, bars, and fine-dining restaurants, offering a picturesque view of the Yarra River. Just a stone's throw away, South Melbourne is known for the famous South Melbourne Market, where you can find fresh produce, gourmet foods, and local artisanal goods. The area also boasts a thriving café culture, with some of Melbourne's best coffee spots found here.

Clarendon Street offers an array of local shops and eateries, making it a great place to explore after a visit to the market.

Docklands: Modern Shopping, Dining, and Entertainment

Docklands is a modern, waterfront neighborhood that offers a striking contrast to Melbourne's historic districts. Known for its innovative architecture, Docklands is home to large-scale shopping centers, including Harbour Town and The District Docklands, as well as a variety of dining options along the waterfront. Visitors can explore the Melbourne Star Observation Wheel, offering panoramic views of the city, or take a stroll along the Docklands Waterfront for great photo opportunities. The neighborhood also offers entertainment options like Marvel Stadium, home to sports and concerts, and a range of bars and restaurants with views of the harbor.

North Melbourne and Kensington: Off-the-Beaten-Path Neighborhoods

For a quieter, more residential experience, North Melbourne and Kensington offer off-the-beaten-path charm. North Melbourne is known for its leafy streets, historic architecture, and vibrant café scene, with plenty of places to grab a coffee or enjoy a casual bite. Kensington, located to the north of the city, is a charming suburb that has maintained its village feel while evolving into a trendy area with a great mix of modern cafes, bars, and boutique shops. The Kensington Village shopping strip offers unique finds and is a great place to explore for those looking to avoid the crowds of the more tourist-heavy areas.

Exploring Melbourne's Parks and Gardens: Princes Park, Carlton Gardens, and More

Melbourne is renowned for its green spaces and parks, providing a perfect escape from the urban hustle. Princes Park, located in the inner northern suburb of Carlton, offers wide-open spaces for picnics, running, and cycling, as well as a serene lake for a peaceful stroll. Carlton Gardens is a beautiful, UNESCO-listed site that contains the Royal Exhibition Building and the Melbourne Museum, offering both history and nature in one location. Fitzroy Gardens, located near the city center, features scenic pathways, a charming conservatory, and the Cook's Cottage, a heritage building that holds historical significance. For a more relaxed atmosphere, Albert Park and Royal Park provide vast expanses of greenery, perfect for enjoying Melbourne's temperate climate.

Melbourne's neighborhoods are as diverse as they are dynamic, offering something for every traveler. From the trendy streets of Fitzroy and Collingwood to the cultural heart of Southbank and the modern appeal of Docklands, each area presents its own unique personality. With plenty of parks, galleries, markets, and dining options, Melbourne's hidden gems are waiting to be discovered, making it one of Australia's most exciting cities to explore.

8.0 Day Trips and Excursions from Melbourne

Melbourne is ideally located for a range of unforgettable day trips that allow visitors to explore the surrounding natural beauty, wildlife, and vibrant local culture. Whether you're looking to immerse yourself in coastal beauty, enjoy a glass of wine, or hike through stunning national parks, these nearby destinations offer diverse experiences. Here are some top day trips and excursions from Melbourne:

Great Ocean Road: Scenic Drives, Beaches, and the Twelve Apostles

One of the most iconic road trips in Australia, the Great Ocean Road is a must-do for those who want to experience some of the country's most stunning coastal landscapes. Starting just an hour outside of

Melbourne, the drive follows the southern coastline and offers breathtaking views of the rugged cliffs, golden beaches, and lush rainforests. Highlights along the way include the Twelve Apostles, a collection of limestone stacks rising majestically from the Southern Ocean, and Loch Ard Gorge, where dramatic shipwrecks have occurred throughout history. Additionally, you can stop off at scenic towns like Apollo Bay and Lorne, explore the Great Otway National Park for rainforest walks, and enjoy wildlife sightings such as koalas and kangaroos in their natural habitats.

Phillip Island: Penguins, Wildlife, and Family-Friendly Fun

Located about two hours from Melbourne, Phillip Island is famous for its unique wildlife experiences, making it an ideal destination for families. The Penguin Parade is the highlight, where visitors can watch hundreds of little penguins waddle up the beach to their burrows after a day of fishing in the ocean. Besides the penguins, Phillip Island offers attractions like the Koala Conservation Centre, where you can spot koalas in their natural environment, and Churchill Island Heritage Farm, a working farm that offers a glimpse into Australia's early colonial life. The island is also home to pristine beaches, including Smiths Beach, ideal for a relaxed seaside day. The island's rugged coastal landscapes and wildlife make it a memorable destination for nature lovers.

Yarra Valley: Wine Tours, Vineyards, and Scenic Views

Just an hour's drive from Melbourne, the Yarra Valley is one of Australia's premier wine regions, offering visitors a chance to sample world-class wines and enjoy beautiful rural scenery. The valley is dotted with numerous vineyards and cellar doors, many of which offer guided tours and tastings. You can explore iconic wineries such as Yering Station, Domaine Chandon, and De Bortoli, each offering a different taste of the region. Beyond wine, the Yarra Valley is home to charming towns like Healesville, where you can visit the Healesville Sanctuary, an Australian wildlife conservation center. For a relaxing day, take in the views of rolling hills and vine-covered valleys, or stop for a gourmet meal in one of the region's boutique restaurants.

Mornington Peninsula: Beaches, Hot Springs, and Hiking Trails

For a more laid-back coastal experience, the Mornington Peninsula is just an hour's drive from Melbourne and offers a perfect mix of beaches, hot springs, and hiking trails. Known for its boutique wineries and peaceful seaside villages, the peninsula's natural beauty is on full display at Cape Schanck and Point Nepean National Park. The Peninsula Hot Springs is a major attraction, offering visitors the chance to relax in natural thermal waters, while Sorrento and Portsea are known for their beautiful beaches and vibrant cafés. Nature lovers can enjoy hiking in the Mornington Peninsula National Park, which has coastal trails with breathtaking ocean views. Whether you're interested in gourmet food, nature, or relaxation, the Mornington Peninsula has something for everyone.

Grampians National Park: Hiking, Wildlife, and Nature Escapes

For those seeking adventure and immersion in nature, a day trip to Grampians National Park offers one of the best escapes from the city. Located about three hours from Melbourne, the park is a haven for outdoor enthusiasts with its rugged mountain ranges, waterfalls, and diverse wildlife. Hiking is a key draw, with trails that lead to spectacular viewpoints such as The Pinnacle and Mount William, offering sweeping views of the surrounding plains. Visitors can also explore the Mackenzie Falls, one of the largest waterfalls in Victoria, and spot kangaroos and emus in the park's diverse landscapes. The Grampians also have a rich cultural history, with ancient Aboriginal rock art sites that offer a glimpse into the area's indigenous heritage.

Wilson's Promontory: Pristine Beaches, Wildlife, and Hiking Trails

For those who love nature and wildlife, Wilson's Promontory is a paradise just a few hours' drive from Melbourne. Known as "The Prom," this national park is famous for its unspoiled beaches, dense forests, and abundant wildlife. With over 50 kilometers of hiking trails, the park offers a range of walking experiences, from short walks to longer treks. Squeaky Beach, named for its soft sand, is a popular spot to relax by the ocean, while Tidal River offers camping and picnic facilities with picturesque views. Wildlife enthusiasts can spot native animals such as kangaroos, wallabies, and wombats. The park's tranquil environment and spectacular scenery make it an ideal destination for a nature-filled day trip.

Conclusion

Melbourne's proximity to a variety of diverse landscapes makes it an excellent base for day trips and excursions. Whether you're driving along the Great Ocean Road, experiencing wildlife on Phillip Island, sipping wine in the Yarra Valley, or hiking through the natural beauty of the Grampians, these destinations offer unforgettable experiences. Each location offers a unique blend of adventure, relaxation, and natural beauty, making them the perfect complement to your Melbourne visit.

9.0 Family-Friendly Activities in Melbourne

Melbourne is a fantastic destination for families, offering a wide range of activities that cater to all ages. Whether you're looking for wildlife encounters, educational experiences, or simply a day of fun and relaxation, the city has something to keep everyone entertained. Here's a look at some of the top family-friendly activities in Melbourne:

Melbourne Zoo and Healesville Sanctuary: Wildlife Encounters for All Ages

Melbourne is home to two remarkable wildlife attractions that are perfect for family visits: Melbourne Zoo and Healesville Sanctuary. The Melbourne Zoo, located just a short distance from the city center, is home to a diverse range of animals from around the world, including lions, elephants, and orangutans. The zoo offers interactive experiences such as close-up encounters with animals and feeding sessions, making it an exciting and educational day out for children.

For a more immersive Australian wildlife experience, head to Healesville Sanctuary, about an hour's drive from Melbourne. This sanctuary specializes in native Australian species, including kangaroos, koalas, platypuses, and emus. The Spirits of the Sky bird show and animal encounters are highlights, allowing families to learn about conservation efforts and indigenous wildlife in a fun and engaging way.

Scienceworks: Interactive Exhibits for Kids and Families

For a blend of fun and education, Scienceworks is a must-visit for families with children. Located in the inner-west suburb of Spotswood, Scienceworks offers hands-on, interactive exhibits that engage young minds in the wonders of science, technology, and the natural world. Kids can explore the Planetarium, where they can embark on virtual space adventures, or visit the PlayPod, a creative area for younger children to experiment and learn. The Lightning Room is another thrilling experience, where families can watch lightning strikes up close and learn about electricity in an exciting way. With numerous exhibits catering to different age groups, Scienceworks is a place where learning feels like play.

Melbourne Star Observation Wheel: A Fun Family Experience

The Melbourne Star Observation Wheel provides one of the best family-friendly experiences in the city, offering breathtaking views of Melbourne's skyline and beyond. Located in the Docklands area, the observation wheel reaches 120 meters high and provides a unique perspective of the city, from the towering skyscrapers to the Yarra River and Port Phillip Bay. The fully enclosed cabins are safe and comfortable for families with young children, making it a relaxing yet thrilling experience. A ride on the Melbourne Star is a fun way for families to bond while enjoying the spectacular views.

Family-Friendly Parks: Royal Park, Fitzroy Gardens, and the Melbourne Botanic Gardens

Melbourne boasts several beautiful parks and gardens that are perfect for families to relax, play, and explore. Royal Park, located near the Melbourne Zoo, offers wide open spaces, playgrounds, and walking tracks, making it ideal for a family picnic or a leisurely day out. Fitzroy Gardens, with its lush greenery, large playground, and attractions such as the Fairy Tree and Cooks' Cottage, is another family favorite. The Melbourne Botanic Gardens, located by the Yarra River, is perfect for nature walks, with plenty of space for children to explore, feed ducks, or enjoy a family-friendly picnic. All of these parks feature playgrounds and peaceful settings, offering a great way for families to unwind in nature.

Indoor Activities for Families: Trampolining, Bowling, and Ice Skating

Melbourne is home to various indoor activities that are perfect for families, especially on rainy days. Bounce Inc. is a popular indoor trampoline park where kids (and adults) can jump, bounce, and enjoy a variety of obstacle courses and activities. For a more competitive family day out, Strike Bowling offers bowling alleys, arcade games, and a fun atmosphere for all ages. O'Brien Icehouse in Docklands offers ice skating, making it a cool way for families to enjoy an active day indoors, with options for beginners and more experienced skaters. These indoor venues provide an energetic and engaging way to spend time as a family, no matter the weather.

Kid-Friendly Cafés and Restaurants: Dining Spots for Young Families

Melbourne is known for its vibrant food scene, and many cafés and restaurants cater specifically to families. Several eateries in the city offer dedicated kids' menus, play areas, or activities to keep little ones entertained. The Common Man in Southbank is a family-friendly venue with a relaxed atmosphere and a great children's menu. The Pancake Parlour, a beloved Melbourne institution, is another spot where kids can enjoy pancakes with creative toppings. Fitzrovia in Fitzroy serves healthy and delicious meals in a welcoming space that's perfect for young families. Many cafés also offer high chairs and children's play areas, allowing parents to relax while their children enjoy a snack or a meal.

Conclusion

Whether you're exploring wildlife at the zoo, enjoying interactive exhibits at Scienceworks, or spending the day in one of Melbourne's lush parks, the city offers a wealth of family-friendly activities that are both fun and educational. From indoor adventures to scenic outdoor escapes, there's something to suit every family's interests and energy levels. With these activities, your visit to Melbourne is sure to be an enjoyable and memorable experience for the whole family.

10.0 Practical Information and Travel Tips

Currency, ATMs, and Payment Methods:

The currency in Melbourne is the Australian Dollar (AUD). ATMs are readily available throughout the city, including in major shopping areas and near train stations. International credit and debit cards (Visa, MasterCard, and American Express) are widely accepted, and contactless payments are common. For smaller purchases, you can also use a Myki card, which works for public transport and some retail outlets.

Health and Safety:

Melbourne is a safe city for travelers. In case of emergencies, dial 000 for police, fire, or ambulance. For non-emergency healthcare, Melbourne has several hospitals, including The Royal Melbourne Hospital and St Vincent's Hospital. Travel insurance is recommended to cover potential medical emergencies and unexpected situations like trip cancellations.

Language and Communication:

English is the primary language in Melbourne, making communication easy for English-speaking travelers. While most people are friendly and helpful, learning a few basic phrases like "Excuse me" or "Thank you" can go a long way in building rapport with locals.

Using Public Transport:

Melbourne's public transport network includes trams, buses, and trains. The Myki card is essential for getting around. It's a reusable smart card that you can load with credit and use on all public transport. You can buy and top up Myki cards at vending machines, 7-Eleven stores, and train stations. For short trips within the city center, the tram system is free within the Free Tram Zone.

Internet Access and SIM Cards:

Many cafes and public spaces in Melbourne offer free Wi-Fi. If you need mobile data, you can easily purchase a prepaid SIM card at the airport or mobile shops, with options from Telstra, Optus, and Vodafone. These providers offer a range of plans for both data and calls.

Sustainability and Responsible Travel:

Melbourne encourages sustainable travel practices. Opt for public transport or hire a bike to explore the city, and avoid excessive plastic usage by bringing a reusable water bottle. Additionally, supporting local, eco-conscious businesses can contribute to the city's sustainability efforts.

Printed in Great Britain
by Amazon